Sept. 9. 1996
Samantha Ash
from
Grandma Hiller
+
Grandpa Davies.

Jennifer of the City

written and illustrated by Corbin Hillam

For Annie and Brad

Copyright © 1990 Concordia Publishing House
3558 S. Jefferson Avenue, St. Louis, MO 63118-3968
Manufactured in the United States of America

Library of Congress Cataloging in Publication Data

Hillam, Corbin.
  Jennifer of the city / by Corbin Hillam: illustrated by Corbin Hillam.

  Summary: The daughter of missionaries describes how she and her family tell
people in the city about Jesus.
  ISBN 0-570-04183-X
  1. Missionary stories. 2. Children of missionaries—Juvenile literature. 3. City mis-
sions—Juvenile literature.
  [1. Missionaries]   I. Title.
BV2087.H4852   1990
266—dc20   89-35419
                                             CIP
                                             AC

1 2 3 4 5 6 7 8 9 10   99 98 97 96 95 94 93 92 91 90

I used to wake up to the sounds of parrots and monkeys calling me out to play. That was in my jungle home.

Now I wake up to the sounds of horns honking, music playing, and shopkeepers calling out their early morning greetings. Now I live in the big city.

Dad, Mom, Josh, and I live on the 10th floor of a high-rise apartment building. The noises are different than before, but it's still my home.

We eat breakfast together, just like we did in the jungle. (I think breakfast is my favorite time of the day.) After we eat, we take time to talk to God about the things we will be doing.

Dad and Mom are missionaries. We ask God to help them tell many people about Jesus. We ask God to be with Josh and me at our new school. I always remember to pray for my friend, Skip, back in the jungle. He flew an airplane and brought us all our food and medicine.

After we pray, we all clean up the kitchen. Now it's time for Dad to go downstairs to the mission. He has many jobs to do.

Every day Dad tells people about Jesus. That's his favorite job. He tells them that Jesus died on the cross to take away all the bad things we do. He also helps people who are sick or in trouble.

Dad gives people food from the food closet at the mission. He says it reminds him of Jesus feeding hungry people. Dad says that one day Jesus gave food to more than 5,000 people. There are lots of hungry people in the city. I bet more than 5,000!

At night Dad teaches a class to people who are learning to speak English. The room is filled with people from all over the world who can speak many different languages.

I like to help Dad pass out paper and pencils. He calls me his teacher's aid. I always hope someone from my jungle home will come, but so far no one has.

Mom set up a day-care center in our mission. She takes care of kids while their parents go to work. Mom is even teaching the children how to read the Bible, just like she did in the jungle! Josh likes to help Mom when he gets home from school.

I have lots of new friends in my neighborhood. Every afternoon we play on the front steps of my apartment building.

On Saturday mornings, Manny comes to our apartment. He helps Dad at the mission. He wants to be a missionary, too.

Today Manny said he would take me to the zoo. I have never been to a zoo before. I can hardly wait!

It's a long way to the zoo. First we walk to our subway station. At the entrance I see a man sitting on the sidewalk, asking for money. Manny stops and talks with him. Manny even gives him some money.

"Manny," I ask, "why is that man asking for money? Is he poor?"

"Yes," explains Manny. "He is sick and cannot work. I told him to come to the mission for help. Then we can tell him about Jesus and how He helps people."

We have to ride the subway all the way across the city to get to the zoo. The subway is a train that travels underground. At first I am scared. I've never seen so many people! Manny says it will be okay.

What a fun ride! But it sure feels good to be up in the daylight again. As we leave the subway I see a little boy selling newspapers. He is smaller than I am! "Manny, isn't that boy too little to be working?" I ask.

"He is awfully young," says Manny, "but he has to work to help earn money for his family. That way they can buy the food they need and pay for a place to live."

Finally we get to the zoo. I am so excited about seeing all the animals!
I race through the gate before Manny can pay for our tickets.

I can't believe there are so many animals living in the city. It's great to
see my old jungle friends!

But before I know it, I have lost Manny. I look all around but I cannot find him! I don't want to, but I sit on a bench and start to cry.

"Hi," says a boy from the other end of the bench. "My name is Simon. Are you lost, too?"

"Yes," I sniff. "My name is Jennifer. This is my first time at the zoo and
can't find my friend." When I think about Manny I start to cry again. But
ust a little bit.

"Hey, that's okay. I get lost here all the time," says Simon. "You've never been to the zoo before? How come?" he asks.

"I have only lived in the city a little while," I say. "I used to live in the jungle."

"Wow, the jungle!" says Simon. "What was it like there? What did you do in the jungle? Did you swing through the trees on vines?"

"Slow down, Simon," I laugh. "The jungle was beautiful. Sometimes I really miss it."

"Well, why did you live there?" asks Simon.

"My mom and dad are missionaries. They tell people about Jesus," I say.

"Oh, yeah? Who's Jesus?" Simon asks.

"You don't know Jesus? He's God's Son. He came to earth and died on the cross to take away our sins. If we love Him and believe in Him, someday we'll get to live with Him in heaven," I explain.

"Heaven! What's that?" Simon asks.

"It's a super place," I explain. "We'll get to play with Jesus and talk to Him all the time. It will be better than the jungle and the zoo," I laugh.

"Gosh, that sounds great!" says Simon. Just then Manny walks up to s.

"Hey, Jennifer where have you been? Do you and your friend want to o see the monkeys?" asks Manny.

"Come on, Simon. Let's go see the monkeys. Then we will help you find your parents," I say.

"Boy, these monkeys remind me of my jungle home. I'm so glad I can live in exciting places like the city and the jungle," I say.

"Jennifer, do you think you would want to be a missionary?" asks Manny.

I smile at Simon. "I think maybe I am a missionary right now, Manny," I answer.

How about you? Can you be a missionary right now, where you live? Ask God's Holy Spirit to help you tell your friends about Jesus' love. He'll help you do it!